In Late Light

Johns Hopkins: Poetry and Fiction
John T. Irwin, General Editor

Poems by Brian Swann

In Late Light

The Johns Hopkins University Press
Baltimore

This book has been brought to publication with the generous assistance of the Albert Dowling Trust and the Writing Seminars Publication Fund.

Printed in the United States of America on acid-free paper
9 8 7 6 5 4 3 2 1

The Johns Hopkins University Press
2715 North Charles Street
Baltimore, Maryland 21218-4363
www.press.jhu.edu

Library of Congress Cataloging-in-Publication Data

Swann, Brian.
In late light : poems / by Brian Swann.
p. cm. -- (Johns Hopkins: poetry and fiction)
ISBN 978-1-4214-0856-9 (pbk. : acid-free paper) — ISBN 1-4214-0856-2 (pbk. : acid-free paper) — ISBN 978-1-4214-0857-6 (electronic) — ISBN 1-4214-0857-0 (electronic)
I. Title.
PS3569.W256I5 2013
811'.54—dc23 2012036070

A catalog record for this book is available from the British Library.

Special discounts are available for bulk purchases of this book. For more information, please contact Special Sales at 410-516-6936 or specialsales@press.jhu.edu.

The Johns Hopkins University Press uses environmentally friendly book materials, including recycled text paper that is composed of at least 30 percent post-consumer waste, whenever possible.

For Roberta, always, with love

Contents

1 *Temenos*

Worlds

Air is empty. It's empty.
We fill it with absence. The piano plays
a few bars, then goes quiet. The sun pounds on
the sea and windows stretch
to breaking point when they will let in
a madman who will tell us what we've all
agreed does not exist.
He walks into a patch of brightness
and fractures into blossom, which is how
he'll be remembered. He will return
years later for the fragments he left
under our skin. With these he'll make more worlds
closer than skin where
the sun gathers itself into raindrops
at the ends of pine-needles, hanging there, heavy,
turning to branches in
night sky so we can touch the moon
and collect the stars and say: "How many
worlds we have!"

In Line

There is a clearing by a certain stone
where images flow and are worth stopping for.
I have stayed there almost all day in silence
until night remembered what belonged to it
and its shadows started to take back its own.
I've found it hard to walk away as starlight
infused daisies and the stone itself began
to feel like a star so, although what I have done
with my life may not be much, for a while
it seemed to be in line.

Rocks

In late light leaves
flick and fish

stare up before
drifting away. I am

not thinking. I'm
watching these

rocks burn at
a thousand points

so you could believe
they have nerves, skin

you can see through,
their freight anguish,

their rhythm patience,
as their shadows fall

and soon they fall
into their shadows

with the sound, if
they could make

a sound, of waves
falling down over

themselves forever

This Place

There is a proper season for stars, and enough
time for the abyss. On this granite floor,
however, nothing is certain, not even the
little song I thought I heard, disembodied,
almost anonymous. It could have been
a poppy head in the display case. Or maybe
a cuckoo. I counted the notes as if counting
was a virtue, and even sang a few notes
in a register useful for grasshoppers,
but it was lost on them. Today, everything
is lost, probably due to the posture gods
used to warm their thighs, which tended
to the crushing of mortals. So now, gigantic
on the wall, their shapes are flickers or fever.
Somewhere may be another world, but I have
chosen this place for the echoes. I stand
behind the lemons on the table as if summoned,
thinking of fishes tossed into a boat. I have
set aside their shiny shadows and will wait to see
how to use them. Whatever they are like
I'll call mine. I have gathered other things
too, indifferent to quality, setting necessity
next to impoverishment. And even if all this
never existed it will appear as something
by which I'll make my way. If when I wake
nothing's there I'll want that too.

Transubstantiation

If we only knew how fireflies are
   long-tailed or short-tailed stars
or even not stars at all but
   lemons dying of thirst, pleading
like sucklings, or soldiers at a
   water-hole smelling of cumin,
feverish on the black wet stones
   so no wonder they look confused
through the flowers and wire
   as little lights go off in their heads
and on their tongues when they
   dive at lightning on the water or
leap up at wandering celestial wheels
   that cast no shadow so they can't
be lost, always where they are going
   in a wide wake, always on the
other side of things, or how they're
   gold of the conquistadores melting
in gouts drifting away, then we might
   know the true substance is not ash
or accident but what's left is still
   the real thing so, though we may not
know what that is, there's no point
   in trying not to catch it.

Temenos

Some forty years ago when I was young
    everything seemed quid pro quo and
feasible even if it wasn't. You could
    grow wise on compulsions or
convert on a whiff. Things aren't
    that way now—at least that's what
I was thinking as I opened the gate
    to a patch of sunlight and stepped into
the shade, of which there was too much,
    but this was the only possible place
for a garden in the woods. I'd dug it out
    from red hardpan and rock around
the house I never thought I'd own,
    filled it in with whatever seemed right,
wood-duff, leaves, potash, kitchen scraps
    and scavenged worms, buckets of manure
hauled from the farmer's field at night,
    whatever came to hand. I never went
to garden school. And now life is heaping
    underground, thrusting up at me, leaping
and heading out like fire, which it is,
    a slow fire, pushing past me out the gate
and fence designed to keep it in,
    caught up in its own possibilities,
even the possibilities of collapse, fruiting
    into capitals and cornices, volutes
and friezes and irregular dancing meters,
    singing a wide-awake sleep of many colors
that envelop and embody you so even
    when you close the gate it's never closed

The Garden

Colors are broken down again
into a collection of breathing. They arrived
as if from nowhere. Some stagger and stay.
Some leave, their sirens giving way to
the flame that sips like a clock. I am
walking around pretending to be
on my way, making edges as I go,
the current curling round me
in ribbons, a tongue flicking in eddies.
There are no lines, just flights, quick
and brilliant, sweeping me up. I wish
for them to stop. They don't.
Everything is rising. Everything is running over.

As If

At my age I should be dead, I think as I walk
among heirlooms under a moon that rocks
and wallows, a ship on the rocks, caught in a swell
that drives her further on, scattering bullion

and moidores. At my age I stay in one place,
and here I am with tomatoes that seem to eat the dark.
I move among them like, I say, mountain water.
They are listening. I am listening. We could be

turning to mountain music as leaves stir, we could
be waiting for the stones to reverberate, stars
start to whistle as they climb over themselves, swinging
about like the seas, and I say, Now you can let me in,

as the fruit moves to its own rhythm, spreading
over the ground, escaping wires and stakes,
mimicking the orange moon, taking it in so
their seeds stir, unbounded as night. They could

be remembering resurrections, being brought back,
while I remember the rockpools of my childhood coast
teeming with fish I reached in for, the threnody
of ocean waters like cornets or conch shells for the

coronation of cardinal or Aztec emperor, *tlatoani*,
or the Buddhas I now walk among, plump, fulfilled,
self-lit incumbents of sun and moon. In their perfume
I move as if forever, as if there were no "as if."

Click Song

For the last few days I've thought I was going mad or about to die, something
going off in my head, my chest, everything caught in the glare of an intense sun,
after my wife of thirty years was told she had cancer, so I've listened to
every word she's said, recording syllable by syllable, in slow motion, every
sound, pause and hesitation, intent as never before, until today, when even
to pass her empty book-basket at the bottom of the stairs is a sign as sharp
as that shotgun's blast, those over-ripe tomatoes left on the vines, the bloated
squash
and the broccoli gone to flower, even the chipmunk's call from the bluestone
slab
we brought from our dead friend Ray's place and laid on top of the wall as if it
grew here,
her call that rebounds from everywhere so if you couldn't see her you wouldn't
know
where she was though sometimes I almost think she's my wife, as when
they stretch out on the deck, one on her back listening to her iPod, the other
on her front listening to the wind, and I tell the chipmunk but not my wife
that I think I'm about to die or going mad as she sits by her burrow dug into
the side of the house and looks at me and I look back, talk to her as if that
can prevent anything bad from happening and as I walk round the garden
I talk to myself to keep calm, and talk to her again whether she's there or not
or to anything within earshot who will listen because today I feel I might die
and I should leave this record in case nobody remembers me except this
chipmunk
who really seems to know my voice and value it and who it seems always appears
when I think of her and often when I don't, who is always in good health
and knows where she's going, who flows down the steps like water, who looks
at me with black pupil-less eyes, singing her healing click-song from the
bluestone slab,
her whole body shaking, putting everything into it, and I try to believe her.

For an Anonymous Thrush

For he can tread to all the measures upon the music
—Christopher Smart, "Jubilate Agno"

For I will consider nobody's bird, this song-thrush
Who is nobody's servant but serves all,
Who for years I have thanked each spring and summer day
Often as I lay on my bed looking out at the trees,
Thinking this and that, and year after year hearing his song,
Immortal bird, as one brief thing, or a few notes, however lovely,
On a string, and then, just a few days ago for the first time
Paying close attention, discovering each phrase to be
Its own bubble and variation, theme of variations,
Quick bell-notes with frays and furbelows, like something
The wind might make if the wind had mind.
For just as recently after, as I say, taking him for granted,
I have watched him closely as he hopped in the small ditch
I dug along my garden to carry off the storm water,
Of which there is a lot, and where he sometimes takes
An earthworm or maybe two for his pains though
It's taken me forever to persuade them to see my plot
For what it is, organic, and make it home, and I'd prefer
He ate the plain brown ones, not those with blue stripes.
For I will consider this bird that flew across my garden
This morning just as the rain began to darken the windows
So they became a mirror, or invisible to him, just a
Quicker way across to the other side. For that was when
I heard the bang and saw small feathers floating
Down silently to where he lay on his right side,
One small black iris-less eye staring up at me
Blinkless, and I thinking, Oh, he's dead. But then,
He'll come around. They often do. They have

Miraculous powers to heal themselves. And so
I waited. But he still lay, and the cold rain
Soaked his feathers. And therefore I will consider
This hermit-thrush who was a good hermit-thrush,
Doing what hermit-thrushes do, nothing spectacular
Apart from his singing, but spectacular nevertheless,
With strong wings and a breast covered with dots like ermine,
A singer of songs and eater of flies that bite the flesh
And caterpillars that eat cabbages, and all manner
of other noxious insects, finding them tasty,
As well as a fat worm or two, which I don't begrudge,
Who bothered nobody for when he didn't sing he was silent
As he went about his days and endured his nights
Without complaint, who blended in, within his heart
Just the wish to be a thrush and make more thrushes
Just like him by singing well.
For he took great joy in his singing, harmonizing
With himself, from the first glance of the glory in the east
Or when dark and cloudy with the threat of rain.
For he kept things straight by keeping on.
For he needed no instruction since he listened carefully.
For he preened his wings as if conferring a blessing.
For he counteracted the Devil, who is Death,
By brisking about his life, though the Devil has
The last word.
For he was an instrument for children to learn music upon,
Though now the house is incomplete and woods barren.
For now the song has broken, gone back to earth.
For this is not good to think on.
For I had said his powers failed.
For the fact that this is not so.
For his powers that earlier I had said failed
Have not. For I checked and checked again until
Two hours and then gave up. And then I checked some more,
The last time rolling back with my hand the tall grass
Where he had fallen. He was not there. The space was empty

And he had gone.
And in the rain a new song like those I'd heard before
But louder, at the same time further off while
Close at hand.
And for I do not have to lie again to my wife and child
When they ask if the bird really did what I said, and did
It all turn out right.
For it did.

A Typology of Birds

> Typology relates to the future, and is consequently
> related primarily to faith and hope, and vision.
> —Northrop Frye, *The Great Code*

I have been here some time where
  single things pull curtains around them
and the loneliest fall into their own breath.
  But in spring I watched water

turn gravity on its head, and saw birds
  quiver like tuning forks. Now
summer's going, when a crack appears
  in the sky they'll fly into it. Circling

stars, they'll spin out to each other
  through nights that give way to them,
following lines to the horizon and then
  over into a nothing like a prayer

they know the answer to, and out beyond,
  whirling away, and I'll know they're
up there, among leave-takings and remainders,
  their solemn eyes a kind of light even

at noon, and the same bells I heard by day
  going on and on, lighter than shapes,
more persistent than appetite, as if one could
  break through to that side and reassure

oneself with renewal and a fresh river
    to cross, which reflects the flight of more birds,
fractured into more by wavelets, and other birds
    severed by the water from their own reflections.

II *Opening the Dark*

Hathor

Life was ordinary then, and I was
ordinary too, a kid. And the cows
were ordinary though each was
a totally different breed, unique,
or no breed at all, picked up
here and there, a mish-mash.
But each had her name, and I
had one too though sometimes
I took theirs, Liz or Vi, Cushie,
Hackie, I had many to choose from,
and sometimes I ate what they ate,
sweet grass stems, or cubed cow-cake,
rich and oily, delicious, and
sometimes I drove them from
byre to burn, walking behind
their hammock-hips, their
easy functions, when summer
nights still depended on stars
that gave us our first gods,
cows and bulls, and which
I could still make out in their
blue-black pastures and watch
until the bombers came for
the mines and shipyards.
After that, milk tasted of fish
and I spat it out for the cows
were now cooped up and fed
fish heads. But they still weren't
safe and I would seldom again
see wide-horned Hathor without
seeing her fields torn apart

and stars shunted aside by
searchlights or blotted by barrage
balloons in nights of sirens and
flames, pummeled by shrapnel.

Moonlight

> Am I here, or am I there?
> —Virginia Woolf, "Street Haunting"

The sting of moonlight is everywhere,
sharp as chipped chert or fer-de-lance,
but the hummingbird of July is still

in my head, swooping in an arc, up
and down, flipping over, whirring,
a shuggyboat at the Spanish City, up

and down, the bombs finished falling,
fathers returning, bunting and union jacks
down, and us kids in December coating

clogs or soles of bare feet with candle-
wax to slide in the playground outside
the doorless school lavs, up and down,

butcher paper and newspapers stuffed
inside shirt or jerkin, happy and relentless
as drunks.

Peel

I read that in this famous person's poems "she searches
for signs of what lies beneath and beyond the self."
Which seemed to me pointless, as if you wouldn't know

whether to paint with egg tempera or eat it. At eighteen,
I came across Tolstoy's "What Is Art?" where he said
an artist is different from other people because instead

of eating an apple he paints it. Even then I thought why
can't he paint it and then eat it, the way at eight, the war
just over, I stood shoeless in line in the snowy playground

where one of the kids was handing out something that turned out
to be small pieces of orange peel, something exotic we'd never
seen before, which I smelled, nibbled, and finally ate for this
poem.

Land of Flint

Snow slopes away to someone going by.
It could be me. There is a whistling like wind

on edges, and a hammering, a pause, then
hammering again in uneven phrases.

Air tilts, and shadows ride up. Spaces
swell then shrink, shimmer like foxfire

so the land's a-glitter, references gone,
anonymous and unfamiliar. I scratch

my name on a rock. Clouds go red as
the horizon wanders, glistening and hollow.

There is a rage here that has lived many lives,
that cuts into things, reminding me of a boy

crawling along a passageway dug out
thousands of years ago in chalk for nodules

of flint to knap keener than a knife, to shape
a being that shapes what it's shaped by.

Correspondences

> . . . the unity in variety,—which meets us everywhere.
> —Emerson, "Nature"

I'm reading Folsom with a view to a poem
about Daniel Boone because last week I remembered
my childhood neighbor Mr. Boone the chemist
who had a shotgun and a pet fox and who looked
like a fox himself, always in brown tweed or
cavalry twill and deerstalker, and who was followed
everywhere by his unmarried daughter May,
red hair streaked gray, whose dead mother was Welsh
like Daniel's wife's kin. But I put the book down,
look out the window and see what seem fresh
fox tracks in the light snow. I whistle, and the
pine boughs whistle back, bounce, go quiet.
I whistle again. Again they move and at my feet
dead black flies drift along the white oak boards.
Things are spare, but focused, consistent, responsive,
and you can tell who you are by where you are,
the way in Hebrew the verb *to be* has no present
tense; it's implied by circumstance.

Opening the Dark

Sweeps had draped the furniture as if
   somebody died. But weeks later
the woodstove's backed up again.
   I dismantled pipes, stripped everything, thrust
my arm along the dark flue into the
   main chimney until, against my hand
I felt solid coke the ball missed.
   Fingers found a hole and entered,
working blind in the dark, pulled away
   some gunk, opened a bit the seal it took
a chisel to smash for cold air to
   rush down my arm like a needle.
Then, for a while, the fire roared like
   my father's madness. My visiting
mother is padding around the house with
   short blind steps. She is ready to go out.
She has tugged her corsets over the belly
   that shaped me, pulled the last flap shut
between her legs, tied herself into a parcel,
   as the stove dies down. Light filters through
the snow-clogged window. Stepping over
   crusted snow and ruts where water stood,
froze and melted, mother takes my elbow.
   I point the flashlight along the rising
narrow path, briefly opening the dark.

Pity Me

That's me eating a fifty-year-old
egg sandwich in the crowded compartment
as Consett's steel mills flash by
and then pointing, mouth full, at
PITY ME. Really, that's the town name.
And that's still me, today, listening to her
ninety-year-old voice whinging from the long faces
of day lilies and tiny heads of lilies of the valley,
her favorites: *You tore me up inside. Down there.*
My mary hurts. I feel a terror I do not understand.
I want to chew her musquash coat to shreds,
her camiknickers and camisole, nylons—
not nylons but postwar painted seams
(*are they straight?*) and dance down
to the devil in the Scottish dancing pumps
she would not let me have and which
I stole and hid with all the rest,
her Pond's cold cream, pink powder puffs
and pink powder, silver-backed
mirrors on silver trays, a leather
nailpolisher and tortoiseshell knicknacks,
and where I hid myself and which,
for all I know, are still there.

Old Men

My mother kneels at a pool
as if to read it. As evening comes
she sees me reflected on the prowl
like the priest at Nemi. We were not
a close family, scarce family at all,
so nothing could go wrong. To make sure
I left early forever, wishing to be clean
as a seabird in the wind. But here I am
watching her read herself in the pool,
a paraphrase of someone. She stands
and points at the thing she sees, which
is not like the real thing at all.
She starts to speak, but before she can finish,
what had been a photo becomes a frame
marked Empty in which faces flash like fish.
Light tilts, water sloshes over her kneeling again,
singing, reciting in a foreign tongue I can't
even hear. It was then I knew she
wasn't my mother. How could she be?
Old men don't have mothers.
What would be the point?

Lily

Heading out down our dusty road
I thought: Who wears cameos today,
or nylons with seams, or powders
her face with a pink puff kept
in a silver case, or wears a veil,
or elbow-length gloves, and who
gathers blackberries and filberts
from the side of the road or bothers
with apples from trees gone wild?
Heading back up our dusty road,
past another abandoned farm,
wondering if the scabby apples
in my pockets were once
Swaar or Sweeting, Niack Pippin
or just plain Pippin, I'm wakened
by gold flecks lifting ahead and
snagging on the telephone wire thin
as the chain with its namesake
enamel lily my mother always
gave me to wear under my shirt
every time I had to do something
frightening or dangerous. I watch
the finches clog the line that
brings her words over thousands
of miles, frightened, old, sick,
alone, "What is to become of me?"
and think because of this
what will become of me?

Mangoes

To even touch the tongue to them's to
taste something like
the eternal, or what could pass
for it, certainly the unique, the not-to-be-
forgotten, but a few too many bites
cloy, which it's
doing now, dripping on this
page that's trying to understand a thing or two
including death, the comedy of death,
which ticks even closer
today, my birthday, August 13,
Venus's Day in the old Roman calendar, so what,
and a few days after my mother died, her last
gargled words over
the water, after "Why don't you come
to see me?" *I love you,* as the seconds and minutes
ticked by, as the clock ticks and chafes now so
I am thinking of converting
to a tree, that white pine
outside my study window, for instance, that was
a stick when I bought this house and now over-tips
the roof, blocking my view
of mountains so I may have to top it
but know I won't since March's ice storm did some
of that for me, and I feel pity, pity
for the tree, so why not
for my mother who brought me into
this world, though if consulted it might have been against
my wishes, but now I'm at the other end
I may reverse positions
though it is not up to me,

as it isn't for the pine that's still pushing upward
with the ambition, maybe, even wounded, of
being a mainmast in
His Majesty's Navy, although there isn't
a navy any more that needs such masts, and to which
we can say "God save," as to my mother sailing
now somewhere out
of light if not of mind or hailing
distance, beyond the transatlantic cable, beyond "I'm sorry"
though I'm not sure what for, and hope she can
forgive me for whatever
I need forgiveness for, as I
forgive her for not being able to be other than she was,
and for saying "I love you" and for me saying
the same when I didn't know
why or what good it did since
words mean something different each time they're said, or
something different to each side, which
is what words were made for,
to be able to say one thing and mean
another, or even nothing at all, which brings me back
to mangoes, whose taste like love can be too much,
its nutritive flesh sicken,
its juices dripping over lips and chin,
the way I guess the blood dripped over the hungry lips
and chin of Odysseus's mother as she lapped from the dish
her son set before her in Hades,
blood that could have been his own,
while the other ghosts flittered about in the twilight, squeaking,
waiting their turn, and Odysseus waited to
find out how he'd get back home.

Moth

in memoriam, LMS (1916–2007)

Feet in the empty barn slip, and a sparrow
flies out of the darkening leaves. You can hear
distant voices and the noise from a stream that builds
its own structure decaying at a constant rate.

Night's shadows grow, cast by a full moon.
As I walk up the hill through air stippled
by fireflies I can see it over my shoulder
lifting in the southeast above the mountain.

When I turn and go back down it too
sinks until it disappears back where
it came from, drawing its shadows in after.
A small white moth floats by my face

and into the blank woods. How can it see
where it's going? How does it know where it is?

Repayment

These muses of nobody else
—Theodore Roethke, "Frau Baumann, Frau Schmidt,
and Frau Schwartze"

Ubi sunt? I know where they are,
the same place they've been for years,
silent and alone. But where there's
burial there's resurrection. Now
the lovely heads of my young
mother's young friends are up
and looking around, a bit dazed,
wondering who I am, much older
than they were when they knew me,
or thought they knew me, assuming,
maybe, I visited simply for the pleasure
of their company, plus tea and cakes,
which I did, of course, but also for
the change Auntie Lily Herdman kept
in a satin purse embroidered with
a dragon always lying open on the sofa.
At Aunt Mary Buddle's little house,
while she made the tea I visited the purse
tucked under the carefully folded underwear
fragrant with lavender sachets in the
living room dresser under the careful eye
of Uncle Ben, her absent bearded sea captain
husband nobody'd ever met. (Once,
talking about him, she got her wedding ring
stuck up her nose.) The coins were a
kind of touch I saved in a glass jar
under my bed where they joined those

from Aunt Vi Thrower at whose
piano stool's scented plushness and
warmth I worshipped after she rose
to go to the little kitchen having worked
up a sweat with "Count Your Blessings" and
"The Floral Dance" whose chorus went
"each one making the most of his chance,"
and "The Song of Love Is a Sad Song"
("don't ask me how I know") and
many others (she'd sung on the BBC).
No one of these ladies had any kids,
save me. The above was my repayment.
And now this.

Ghost Image

My mother enters with two old ladies, "Do you know how
to turn the TV on?" "No," I say, turning on a wildlife program
while sprawling on the armchair. My father walks in,
his young man at his side. "Keep your wings in," he says

as he digs me in the ribs. Why can't he just stay away,
puff his big cigars in hell, dig into steaks big as those he'd
seen New York firemen eating in the '30s and envied all his life?
Why can't he just drown again in his own "Cutty Sark"? I go

back to the Galápagos Islands where Darwin is collecting a plant
whose digestive juices work like a man's. He is observing the
start and end of things, how each is trapped, how correlations
are almost numberless, how there are only a few forms and

almost endless variations, which makes me think we are
laws whose workings are left to chance as the screen flutters,
on the blink again, just a flickering ghost image floating in it
and voices fading, which I can't turn off.

The Amazon

> A new world is only a new mind
> —William Carlos Williams

I have decided to be happy in a new world
where even my father's hateful face has a place.
Here strangers come together like rain
and beds are full of wisecracks; where
I can reinvent and improvise trees,
and when alarms cry nothing bad happens.
When I am done all this will be a forest,
permanently surprised, intuitive and lovely,
and if there are memories they will be good,
my aunt, for instance, his sister, cutting him
when he came at me for daring to look him in the face.
It was she, normally timid, who took off
almost all her clothes and embarrassed everyone
by slinging them out the window—*What I'll do to you*
if you don't leave the boy alone—where they fell into
February 1950 which is in my mind still on the cover
of my *National Geographic*. That's me there too
beside the Amazon, a naked boy, brown
and befeathered, bow and arrow in my hand,
my father tied up. When I'm ready, I'll climb
out of that picture. But where will I go? I'm happy here,
waiting for my aunt who is, I'm sure,
already taking off what little she has on,
and is about to climb in to sort him out again.

The Knife

I found it at the very back of my desk drawer among medals,
dingy ribbons, old coins, dust. On the silver cardboard box-lid,
"W. R. Humphreys & Co. Ltd., Sheffield, England, Pocket Knife,

'Radiant,' " and inside reclining calm and beautiful as "Olympia,"
on a coffin of cotton-wool or cloud-bed, twin blades folded
into mother-of-pearl. My father gave it to me, not sure what else

to do with it. Maybe his father gave it him, and his him, ages ago,
all doubtless hard men of few words, and those sharp. It lies pristine,
an illegible date like cuneiform scratched on the back of the box.

I pick it up, the size of a sardine. The longer I look at this
descendant of Mousterian or Clovis the bigger it seems.
I open up a blade, test an edge, draw a bloodline across my palm,

and listen. "*Knife,*" it says, the "k" sounded, guttural tenuis. I fold it up,
lay it in the box, stick it in the back of the drawer where I hear it
mutter *clod, cunt, cretin, krippen,* and I try again to forget it's there.

The Obsidian Mirror

Last night I watched a dog fox
digging under the holly bush.

He stopped and looked up at me
with ice-green eyes. Father is

planning to leave for good. He sits
at the kitchen table, staring ahead.

Something is howling under my
bedroom window, but when I look

out there is only grass sparking
like bits of heaven's broken dome

and above only a blackness where
you'd think was intense heat and light,

the sun being there, but which is
in fact colder than can be imagined,

and yet this cold gives off a light
that accounts for us, bouncing off

the obsidian mirror back of it all.

Beyond

Why was the only stroke
 he taught me no stroke

at all, but the dead man's
 float? What thoughts,

as I train some of the
 tardier scarlet runners

up the strings where, at the top
 others have already pushed

between deck planks into
 freer air, sitting there, little

green buddhas—*gáte, gáte . . .** As
 he held one hand under me

I tried to relax. *Put your head back.*
 Trust me. And when I opened

my eyes I was floating, nothing
 under me, and above a clear sky

with one cloud I followed back to
 my father standing on the riverbed

**The Heart Sutra*, Gautama Buddha's words at enlightenment: "Gáte, gáte, pāragate, pārasamgate," "Gone, gone beyond, gone utterly beyond."

like the Granta's god, as I slowly
drifted away between pollarded willows,

the same place where he'd learned
to swim, but with no one to help.

The Drowned Boy

I searched into the night, diving down
through the moon at the center of the lake

where weeds floated and there among
the stems my hands touched something

and I pulled it out and headed up
breaking the surface into the moon and

drew the child along backward
on his back and the moon took his face

so there was nothing there but it was still
my face that took everything in and reflected it,

the sky and himself and the lake and me
trying to save what could not be saved.

Night Sky with Figures

My wife sits reading. I slip out quietly. In the cold
I pick out stars I know, then link others in loose
and dangling loops, myths and monsters, and

suddenly I'm beside my father who's talking as if
I wasn't there and stars his own invention, like
the device for sharpening blades he came up with

just before disposables hit the scene, or as if stars
were his to collect and keep like the eggs he preserved
in pails of isinglass opaque as semen, brittle as the

condoms he had me pick out of the soil he got from
the sewage farm to feed his roses. Finally he's among
worlds he always knew were populated. *Have to be.*

Stands to reason. Look at all the stars. They could be
here among us and we wouldn't know it. They're more
advanced than us. They could teach us a thing or two.

Indeed they could. I tack together a constellation for him,
a new Cygnus I push off so it sails away, off into the aimless
cold wastes of space, trailing its own myth, its own story.

The Stranger

I pick up a feather that blew in through the
open window, barred, flat-topped, owl, which
they say makes the owner invisible. So I take it
with me to my study, and get to work. The calls

of crows are the only break in the silence until
I hear them coming up the stairs, the same thuds
and grunts and curses each day, voices I want
to be shot of that follow when I slip up here,

expecting me to feed them. They wheeze and gasp
for they're old or sick or both, especially the
white-haired geezer who sits in the corner in his
blue wool bathing suit sticking hairpins in his ears

to draw out the wax, or staring into a hand mirror
to squeeze the pores in his nose covered with red
spider veins, popping out the gunk. He's the stranger
who is always there, even if I don't look, making me

(hands over ears) his confidant, giving me his take
on everything, the moon, stars, cars, women and life
in general—"I'm right, right?" he whines. "Write it
down. It's worth something. Fork out. Fuck off.

Nothing for nothing. Money doesn't grow on trees.
I can't support you forever." He's always younger
than me and getting younger, older than me and
getting older. Always here. Here forever. Always.

III *Ghost Dance*

Grandfather Clock

The hour lifts. Rime clips
   the railing like a reliquary
circling, and sleeps. There's
   an albatross's wing wide as the
clouds so you can understand
   sky's limits though you've never
seen an albatross, imagining it as a
   a giant seagull, all appetite. The bird
falls, snow takes over. I think I hear
   the beat of oars, or their echo.
I would like to interact with everything,
   retract, strip, and start again. How
impersonal it all is out there,
   a grain in the sky like granite.
A sound in the hall, the grandfather
   clock I've taken with me each time
I've moved though I only had one
   grandfather and him dead
over fifty years. Its chiming
   can be ignored but without it
there'd be nothing for that
   corner. I wind it up each week
hoping it will stop and I can
   clear the corner out, clean it up,
take everything to the dump
   ("Recycling Center"). One large hand
lags a bit, a number or two droops,
   the trunk's big as a bridal chest
with room for a bed of flowers.
   When I lose the key I always
find it again. I've tried not winding.

It seems to wind itself, calling my bluff.
The minute hand stays still, twitches,
hesitates, then jumps the gap. I remember
as a child wondering what was
in that timeless empty space
when my grandfather who one moment
I was watching in the garden
weeding, the next comes in
and drops dead at my feet.

The Pit

I.

Grandfather goes with canaries and blind ponies down
the mines where God's lamp spins on his helmet.
In the evenings, stripped to the waist, he washes in
the kitchen sink. After supper, in the parlor among
small glass animals and wax flowers, he injects himself
with insulin, then knocks back a bottle of Newcastle Brown.

II.

He gave me a book with the faces of sinners eaten by fire,
told me stories of the Devil met down the pits, a black man,
pretty as a curl, collecting souls. Thunder, he said, was
the Devil dancing overhead in his clogs, clogs the miners wore
for work or for clog-fights that left their shins black
as the coal that coursed through lungs and veins.

III.

One Hogmanay the Devil knocked at our door with a lump
of coal in his hand. I screamed. "It's only Uncle Jack,
first-footing," said my grandmother. But I'd looked
through the burnt cork and saw that face crushed by
his motorbike, blood flowing down the Coast road
into the gutter and the blackness below.

Rag and Bone

A toy trump summons us, then "Rags and bones,
old rags, old bones" the way they used to call
in city streets "Bring out your dead" and pile them up
on carts to haul away, and you come running for a world

where in return for cast-off clouts and bleached soup bones
you get the wonder of a goldfish in a jar, a sticky
handful of black bullets, a small toy or, if there is nothing,
that is what you get, and the sense that things have somehow

balanced out as you watch him trundle on down steep
Crow Bank, his call a crow's we trail across the burn in spate,
over ground ochre-red with pit fires still smoldering beneath,
and there we lose him in the silence, and drift back up.

Time Saver

> To have no-mind is to deliver all things
> —Hui-Chung

On certain days light's
    the light in things, flowing
from instead of leaking
    out, and mind's no-
mind, like this morning
    when the photo on my
shelf flares up, grandparents
    in pony and trap, she
eighteen, he older by a bit,
    everything looks poised,
even the pony seems borrowed
    from a plinth, and I think
how good that they can see
    me now, not the boy they
raised who up and left—
    oh, what I'd give to get
in there with them, I his age,
    she as I never knew her,
as she could never have known
    herself, or me, the now me,
have her reach back, flexible
    as time, as the whip she balances
in her right hand, back to the
    small rear door and let me in
to a time beyond regret or blame.

Floating

in memoriam, Raymond G. Brown

The old white pine we'd cut down still lay head west.
The tarp lay crumpled where he'd dropped it.
Under the trumpet-vine sat a clump of his hair he'd
cut that summer. A plate of ice on the grass resisted rain

and my face swung in the glass sides of the bird feeder.
In the sleeping loft I found a tin box with faded photos:
him in uniform astride the turret of a Sherman tank, smoking,
a baseball with best wishes from Spud Chandler,

undeveloped negatives of a blonde in profile, and a trick
photo of him and his wife of one year, the cancer in her
even then, rising a quarter-century back over a balcony
of the Empire State, about to float over Manhattan.

Light

in memoriam, RGB

No point in reproaching the dead.
Everyone stays, and comes out of you.

And sometimes there's a way back
to them, even if the path goes in wide loops

past the unweeded garden, past strips
of black cloth stuck through the chicken wire

to keep off the birds, past bare bushes and—
a tree is suddenly flooded with light that

seems to come from nowhere and suffuse
like a flame behind a waterfall before gathering

itself in like the ball of light his mother
as a girl in Russia saw enter the house through

one door and float out through the other.

The Lake

in memoriam, RGB

He has come back to walk through the deserted rooms. He smells the shadows,
moves around like melting ice on windows while the room fills with light.
And suddenly he remembers everything: streets of the Bronx, the Grand
Concourse,

his Russian mother's teas of grasses and herbs. He calls her name, but she
is very far away, a girl watching a ball lightning float in through the window
and out the door. Looking out his window he sees birds in a great fan widening

over the Catskills, first one sway, then another, blessing the small brown house
on Ohayo Mountain where someone has come by and swept the floors, polished
mirrors, stood up on its point the cello he could never learn to play. Listen:

water is rolling over cliffs in great shimmering bolts. He watches shadows
of smoke over snow. His eyes move like amazed animals through a world
so suddenly removed until a new sun rises over stone walls. He rises too

and walks among them. Landscapes reflect off his skin. The sun lengthens.
From way off here, you can see a man, now little more than a fatherless boy,
step out into the center of an unmarked lake.

Identity

in memoriam, RGB

They wouldn't let me identify the body. When his two
nephews came downstate the city morgue was closed.
For a week they shuttled up and down, never arriving

on time. So the body just lay there until they phoned to say
they'd seen it, but couldn't be sure. "What do you mean,
not sure?" I said. "Well, he was, well, we don't want to go

out on a limb." He lay there another week until they named him,
alone as when he'd died in his East Tenth walkup railroad flat,
top floor, under a thin asphalt roof that bubbled in summer

and in winter, more than once, collapsed. After Thanksgiving,
when neighbors complained of the stench, the super called
the cops who found him slumped over his desk. "The cats

were going wild," he said. "You wouldn't have recognized him.
I knew him as a tall white man not a short black man.
They had to peel his face off the wood."

The Waves

Where's the past? It's here or nowhere
—Italo Calvino, *Invisible Cities*

Awake I dream . . .
—Hannah Green, *The Dead of the House*

in memoriam, Hannah Green (1927–1996)

We level out and all's well. I reach for the *Times* stuffed into
the seat-pocket and flip through, stopping at an article on his
"blockbuster" retrospective at the Venice Biennale, with a photo
and him remarking of the huge sign "emblazoned" with JACK

WESLEY, "That is really something, isn't it?" Where has he been?
Where have I been? I sleep, and then we are over the water at La Guardia.
I fold the paper to take with me, remembering where I put Jack's cartoon
he gave me for *The Very Last Fish*, and am about to stand up when

I realize I've taken off my pants. Is this really happening? Waves
are lapping at my ankles and I'm with him and Hannah after our drive
south to visit one of her Columbia students near Livorno arriving late,
and the four of us dashing to the empty beach, shedding our clothes

and heading into the dark sea and Hannah, bountiful Hannah,
laughing over the surge, is letting go of Jack's hand, then turning
to beckon me further in, but I'm holding back, afraid of what I cannot see,
what might be hidden under the waves that do not frighten her.

Ghost Dance

in memoriam, Anthony Burgess

The times are delightful, but always fated
to be long ago, like a pitcher of roses, and
shadows are lovely, lovely in themselves as essence,
hence this perfect fragrance in the air today,
perhaps cherry blossom since in Japan, I'm told,
the character for heaven is Fuji reflected in a pool, calm and still,
quiet unchanging perfection, which makes me wonder
what the character for life is and how you get it
to stay still long enough to write down, and what
it means when you fix it, and I remember asking
my old friend Anthony Burgess, now shadow and
reflection himself, "What do you mean?" when he said,
"Don't do that!" as I spun about stomping hundreds
of roaches that spilled from weeks of unwashed stuff
in the dishwasher I'd opened to get a clean cup
for the "mother-in-law tea" he'd just brewed,
black and bitter but fragrant with Bushmills
from a case an admirer sent. "That's life!" he roared.
But I couldn't stop hopping about to shake them off.
"D'you know," I panted, not quite changing the subject,
"You have the same English name as Wovoka,
the Paiute Prophet, founder of the Ghost Dance?"
One hand holding his cup, the other in the air,
a shadow on the wall, beating *contra punctum*,
he slowly joined the dance.

Strange Flowers

In a wheelchair a little old lady who's slid
from straight forgetting to flinging food against walls
to pinching the nurse who was trying to kill her,
"filthy Russian bastard," till she bled, to pinching
punching and scratching anyone who came near,
"I want to scratch everyone," to singing "The Star-
Spangled Banner" over and over, she who never sang,
to just sitting and shrinking, flat eyes staring at me,
she who divided the world into fools and bastards
and I'm still not sure which I am in eyes alien as those
of Grays who do unspeakable things to you in
flying saucers, now and then taking Ensure through
a straw the way a weevil sucks sap, sometimes
moving her hands over her face to dislodge the webs
or maybe she wants to speak so I move closer, but she's
looking, a flicker, a mayfly's wing, past me to her
daughter's face as if she wants to land there, and her
wishing-puff of white hair stirs in a breeze through
the window open a crack a bee slips through, and I recall
something about bees remembering a human face if
they are tricked into thinking we are strange flowers.

Longinus on the Bowery

All memories are echoes
—Grace Schulman

While Grace "hunched in a corner seat" watching Auden with his
Selected Poems on her lap and storing up for "Notes from the Underground:
W. H. Auden on the Lexington Avenue IRT," I could have been

on St. Mark's Place, going to work and glancing up at the plaque
that said he'd lived there, joking to myself "What a place to live,
half way up a wall," and thinking he and I must have crossed paths

many times but I never saw him, unlike Ginsberg who I saw all over the place,
last time through the window of his favorite Chinese restaurant
on the corner of 13th and 1st, razed just after his death for the still

unfinished apartment house I pass each day often humming in my head
like today when it was "The splendor falls on castle walls" and remembering
at seventeen working in Heffer's Bookshop in Petty Cury, both places

long since razed, and that summer selling Benjamin Britten and Peter Pears
copies of Tennyson and Wordsworth, and a year or so later deciding
I was at least partly responsible for the haunting "Serenade," and

as I continued on down 1st I began to remember how I sold Vaughan Williams
a copy of Housman, later to credit myself for his lovely setting of
"Is My Team Plowing" (and the rejoinder "No, it isn't"), and while

whistling it through my teeth, ignoring glances of passersby, recalling
how I'd sold Thomas Tallis the original copy, since lost, of whatever text
he used to compose "Spem in alium," that marvelous forty-part motet

to transport me forever when, in college, I sang in one of the eight
small choirs scattered throughout King's Chapel, and, after turning right
onto St. Mark's, glancing up at number 77, walking on until turning

left toward the Bowery I heard Longinus say the soul is filled
with exultation and delight as if it had given birth to the very thing
it had heard, and then I thought up poets to have them say memory

is the moth's feathery antennae that snags and absorbs bits of air's
brightness, turning it echoic in the weave, dilating specters, navigating
a resonance in no need of originals, creation's holy place. It's all on you.

Loneliness

Like a voice drifting across low damp ground
    it is always there. I have whole files
on the subject. There is nothing more to know.
    My name hangs like a sign outside an old inn,
a painted figure for illiterates, blown to and fro.
    Last night I had a dream of finally falling in love
with a girl I used to know but couldn't recognize,
    whose face gradually morphed into someone
I'd known years before that and put up with
    her crazy cats and pretentious lefty friends,
a child snatched away at birth by his father
    and taken to Germany, her sister and awful family
with fake aristocratic Hungarian names, De-this
    and De-that, an uncle who praised Hitler, and a mother
who looked exactly like Eva Braun, who talked incessantly
    through a terrible overbite. This was what passed
for my deep and final love. There was no way out.
    So, today, I sit upstairs on a day that's dropped
30 degrees in July. I'm stuck. The sound of my radio
    filters through the closed door. My hand reaches
down to pat the invisible dog, calm the invisible child.
    I try to think in a foreign language, one I used to know,
even dream in. The wind is stirring up trees to a frenzy,
    but the chimes on the deck are silent and still.
It must have managed to avoid them, somehow
    sweeping round, so it's the silence of bells I hear.

Tropical Fish

The moth still storms the screen, but
  the killdeer has gone, echoing over the field.
During the night the tip of the hurricane's tail
  lashed across the roof and I wake again with
my head full of arguments no one can win.
  I make no concessions to myself. This is
my trade, opposites. The simplest things
  become complex, and I get nowhere.
Everything becomes speculation, parabolic,
  bending back on itself, floating over
the void, which, we're told, is "eternally
  generative." So I rise and wait, watching
the tropical fish, which are absolutely clear.
  Praise yellow. Praise blue. Praise red
and all colors inbetween and outré too.
  But what's left? Is it vital to be so visible?
Or where they come from do they disappear
  in colors broken and blended? And where
do they go? Oh, tropical fish, translucent
  immediate as azurite or tourmaline,
acute as the diamond's echolalia,
  as I watch, I become invisible, flow
out of myself into the colors of
  loneliness, vivid as the fish.

Firmament

I have Arcturus circled on the wall chart.
  I like the name, but still can't spot him
easily or hunt him down. I look in
  his direction as the sky wheels half-
over then hardens into distance, and
  drops. You'd think I could find him
by now, but you get lost up there in all
  that cold space. I live in Vega Valley
in New York but can't locate the Vega
  in Lyra for sure. I've been trying to
find the names since I was a kid, but
  Charlie's Wain, Orion and his belt,
Polaris and maybe Mars (or Venus)
  is about all I've managed to retain.
Still, I study the chart on the wall,
  but there it all stays, facing the window,
the woods and the sprawl I call
  my garden where each year in some
remote corner or compost pile I find
  something new that sends me to the bookshelf.
That's how I found Joe Pye (six-foot weed
  and Indian doctor), Jimsonweed (high times
in Jamestown), Arethusa ("in wanton
  Arethusa's azure arms"), as well as
phlox, pogonia, dodder, madder, foamflower,
  squawroot (for menstrual cramps), poke
("few have superior powers to poke"—
  skoke/coakum/pokan), puccoon, mocassin
flower, senega (good for snakebite), crazy
  trumpet weed, fabulous milkweed ("I shall
possess the field"), or who could forget

the sexy butterfly pea (clitonia mariana),
or the hot arsesmart? Here I have them all,
and they have me. At night we sleep together,
under the steep curve of my skull.

Over the Moon

To keep time is to remain in time, so
I whistle and sing snatches of old songs
in the kitchen where I'm happy,

throwing together my rat-tat-tat-touille
with whatever's ripe in the garden,
ennobling it all with handfuls of basil.

Memoirs of Hadrian lies on the chair,
but books are graves. No books for me,
no recipes either. I'm making it all up

as I go along. It's not my book anyway,
it's my wife's. Now is party time.
Par-tay! Par-tay! Just us two. Here,

put on a funny hat. Try this squash blossom
for size. Here, hang these beans from
your ears. Look what a big zucchni

I've got! At my age any pleasure is
worth having. The body's still built
for it, the way the trees round here

are built to hold her, the full moon, which
they release bit by bit so she climbs
over the house where she stands still,

taking up the whole sky, drawing it
into herself so there is only light
and nothing else over the moon.

IV *Making It Out*

The Rill

The mountain is a pattern that
whirls, its brightness the absence
of absence. Walking here is not easy.
Once in, there seems no end. It's
dark, but some light's saved in
melting snow along the stream
where a water ouzel runs and
vanishes. Underwater, he looks
like something burning in a high
bright window. The wind weaves
back to its source and out again,
going past me past the old growth
of huge pine the clear-cut forgot
past patches of dark past cracked
and broken things and back into
those things so they seem whole,
cues and slews like thought itself
of which this is the thought, the way
the rill contains itself, overrunning
slabs and rearing back, its clamor
in the quiet an expression of that quiet,
its clarity what it lives on and gives rise to,
allowing itself to be anonymous
whatever we call it, faster and faster,
its freedom restraint, always ahead of itself
in the forefront of falling and falling
over, moving forward in place.
I follow its pulses that deny themselves
the higher and deeper I trek, finally
leaving me alone in the center
of where there is no center.

The Gods

Out the open window light
is everything, seedpod and leaf,

stone, trunk and wall, until
the storm flashes its thousand

flashing cymbals. Here is where
the gods come in. You cannot

unthink them as you stand
in the rout and then in the

aftershock of silence where
you can hear at once the clatter

of pebbles in the stream and
eternity's dark whoosh, the voice

of the scuppernong and whispers
of the rising Pleiades whose

breath is frost spreading
to the tink of tambourines.

The Whistler and His Dog

I steal out to see stars
   multiply. If I breathe now
I'll crack a rock,
   bring the whole thing
down on my head. But I breathe
   and hold still, watching as
children slide past Sirius
   down steep slopes, brides scattering
bouquets, tumbling fruit turning
   back to seedtime. It could be
anything. Put what you like
   up there. I had planned
to photograph this shower
   but there is something comic
about the cosmic. So I set off
   under a falling sky, laughing
and stumbling in the dark,
   whistling "The Whistler and His Dog."
I have no dog and can barely
   hold a tune. But I keep going.
This is what I mean.

The Feather

This blue feather from the nest should be a light to see by
        as I turn it around and read off azure, lapis,
lazulite, linarite, tourmaline, sapphire, and
        so on, but each word and angle's undone by the next
so nothing sticks, telling me nothing except
        that loveliness is trapped and refracted for me
to play with, altering with my look, and I'm
        drawn in to where there are no directions,
no frames, just articulation that seems endless,
        even excessive, vivid hunger generated
by emptiness, where color's just abundance
        of broken light, catching, snagging, slipping,
a shaking of the morning star by the wind that
        opens the sky again to blue that is no color
but an idea that limits space and gives us cover.

Making It Back

I left when a rose flush
on the snow started
the whole thing again and
didn't turn back till,
moonlit, I was walking
through a subzero night,
the world's frequencies low
as I stopped to listen,
then followed some moon-
deepened marks like braille
going in and through me but
I was lost, soon reduced to
prayers even if they were
only notes to the self.
Snow on bushes collapsed
as I pushed through. Bones,
bones, and more bleached
bones, trees. I tried to
push ahead of myself to
prove I was going forward
even if I didn't know
if forward was the right
direction, remembering that
in some of the cultures that
were wiped out round here
the past was in front and
the future behind, but hoping
I could come out the other
side by sheer persistence,
along coordinates of guesswork.

Making It Out

All over these mountains are huge stone walls, piled up by men
With oxen, tackle, crowbars, and brute will. Trees grow right
Through them, and they still stand. When you hike these woods
They come in at all angles, out of nowhere, cross and re-cross,
Holding whole hillsides up, tracing some invisible plan,
Giving you something to go by. But try following and likely
As not you'll stop and look around and say *Where am I?*
Or realize you could be back where you started and so
You have to pull yourself together again and set off, faster,
In a different direction but where the walls still look the same,
Hoping to make it out before it gets too dark to see.

Strangeness

> Trees, it is your own strangeness . . .
> —Ted Hughes, "Trees"

One of the twin maples that rooted over a century ago in our stone wall,
"line tree," the locals call them, is down. It was always there for me,
cows and horses, birds too, but in its fall took with it part of the wall
and the top strand of barbed wire. The horses are nowhere to be seen

and the cows don't seem to notice. There are other shade trees, even
the remaining twin, and, if they wanted they could make like Bailey,
the adventurous heifer who followed the deer over the wall and into
our woods. But no. As dusk falls to the music of metal ear-tags, they follow

their leader at a fair clip back down to the barn. That tree had been leaning
too far out for years, its main branch twice as thick as a man's waist,
the inside rotted out to duff for my garden, just waiting for a storm
big enough to shake the roots in the shallow soil. And now I'm looking

at it from different angles from either side of the wall, even walking on it,
trying to put things in perspective, take it all in. Parts are still green, and
at the top gooseberry bushes are growing in a crotch. Parts are dust, parts
the planks of a sailing ship with scars like the suckers of a giant squid.

There's so much going on, it's bigger than just "tree," or me, and yet it's
not quite "here" nor "there," it's somehow absent or elsewhere. How to get it
straight? How to ask the right questions so it doesn't all come out as if it has
no mind to call its own, as if there are no other minds, as if it's all my fault?

The Horses

As I reach across I'm
taller than the backs
I stroke before they'll move
away for as good a reason
as they stayed, down
the steep hill that's
their meadow of thin grass,
more thyme and rock
than grass, brambles and
this stone wall I'm standing on
that for a while keeps us
all together, I and these horses
so large they'll leave behind
their silhouettes as mountains,
where now as I stroke their
huge heads and necks like pillars,
gentle muzzles and soft mouths,
they stand so still under the great maple
that I can hear them breathe
and I talk to them as if they
could understand more than
I can, as if they don't know
that what I'm saying to them
has no other purpose than
to keep them with me and
me with them here until
I have to turn carefully
around on these loose stones,
step down and find my way
back through the darkening woods.

The Cricket

A raw sun, just
what it is, scrapes
the last few stars
off the sill. Smoke
and dust drift up but
I open the window wider and—
Listen: something is
cutting us off. Something
is chasing away our lives.
Then out of the gray
a cricket arrives that looks
put together from spare parts.
It sits on the sill beside
the iron lamp and starts
to tune up, a few harsh notes,
and then music as if he
cared a lot, or not at all.

The Sky

If a twig snaps overhead, the blood
    rushes through my face. Seeds
of the milkweed still cling to
    their keel. I pull, then release.
Wind swirls the plumes away.
    One, seedless, rises higher than
the spruce with the winter sun
    like a window in it till it becomes
sky. Under pines, grouse step
    in slow motion into a dreaming
land where the air tightens to dark
    and stars are tossed into the sky
by careless Coyote saying, There,
    do what you want. Their light
blues the wood. Snow-squalls open
    before and close behind me. Orion's
three belt studs bar the south. I return
    and enter the house; stand and listen.
The whole sky is resting on the roof.

How I Understand Eternity

Organisms evolved colors before
    there were eyes to see them.
I take a look before floating
    to the Cretaceous where colors
are now butterflies and beetles
    shaping themselves to flowers
of sassafras and magnolia. Their
    scents fill my mind while night
starts to warp round me and a
    rabbit in the doorway pauses
by a half-eaten apple. I watch
    the lamplight's clear pool
on the ancient pinewood planks
    fall through cracks and knotholes
onto the lives of mice as starlight
    filters through the window
and falls on me.

Tableau

Rack to clouds, body gleaming he
leaps like water across the red-dirt

road, and freezes, heraldic, a
tableau in porphyry for a fountain

or a spring like the one at Nauplia
that restored youth and virginity, or

at Epidaurus where you drank, dreamed
and were cured, or the Cyaneaen spring

where you read your answer in a mirror
let down to almost touch the water, or

here where you can almost touch before
he flows like a dream into dark rainy woods.

Magdalenian

This land's pulse
is silence, an ecstasy
drawing me out and
up to this wide mountain
pasture where I stand
still as the stone
wall while five deer
drawn with quick
clear strokes cross
under the horizon
as if they'd just
stepped off a
Magdalenian wall
into a sketch of
scattered boulders
and hardhack on
hooves sharp as the
scents they release
from thin grass and
dry thyme, before
melting back into
the silence that
shaped them.

Masks

Tracks make the invisible present.
A mountain wears trees. The trees

wear sky. The sky wears clouds
so we can see how it moves.

The wind is plumed, bringing
three deer into the clearing to drink.

They are cobalt. They are silk
of the stream bubbling through

ice-arches. They are not deer
any more than the sparrow-size

owls who fly about at evening
are owls. They are souls. They are

still full of light so you think
you can see them.

Cetus

We who are used to daily things
are not used to this, whales

glistening as light falls across them,
silencing itself. They do not seem

to move as we stand in the sun's
monotone, the late hour hammering

itself flat while a locust signals
faintly and a finch goes off

in small arpeggios. Even after
the whales have gone we still

stand there, and they reappear falling
through the universe as the sea

sways shut, and a lost bee lands
on my arm, twitching its gold thighs.

Acknowledgments

Some of the poems in this collection have appeared, sometimes with different titles, in the following journals:

AGNI	"Hathor," "Strangeness"
American Literary Review	"Rocks"
Boulevard	"How I Understand Eternity"
The Hopkins Review	"Strange Flowers," "The Pit," "Identity," "Cetus," "In Line"
Hotel Amerika	"Pity Me"
The Iowa Review	"Lily"
ISLE	"A Typology of Birds," "The Rill"
Michigan Quarterly Review	"The Waves"
New England Review	"Transubstantiation"
New Letters	"The Drowned Boy"
Ploughshares	"Loneliness"
Poet Lore	"Moonlight," "Temenos"
Poetry	"Peel," "Old Men," "The Lake," "This Place"
Poetry East	"Firmament"
Poetry Northwest	"Opening the Dark"
Prairie Schooner	"Correspondences," "Making It Back"
Raritan	"The Cricket," "The Horses"
Salmagundi	"Grandfather Clock"
The Southern Review	"Land of Flint," "The Knife," "Longinus on the Bowery"
Southwest Review	"Worlds," "The Whistler and His Dog"
Stand	"Repayment," "Beyond," "Ghost Dance," "Mangoes," "For an Anonymous Thrush," "The Feather," "Tropical Fish"
Terrain.org	"The Garden"
Western Humanities Review	"Tableau"
Wild Apples	"Light"
The Yale Review	"Masks," "The Sky"

Earlier versions of "Old Men" and "Amazon" appeared in *Autumn Road* (Ohio State University Press, 2005).

About the Author

Brian Swann was born in Wallsend, England, in 1940. He received his B.A. and M.A. from Queens' College, Cambridge, and his Ph.D. from Princeton, where he also taught. In 1972 he moved to Manhattan to teach at the Cooper Union, where he is currently Professor of Humanities. He is the author of five collections of short fiction, eight collections of poetry, five books for children, and a number of volumes of poetry in translation. He has also edited several collections of Native American literature, the most recent of which is *Sky Loom: Native American Myth, Story, Song*, from the University of Nebraska Press. His work has been published in many anthologies and journals including *The Iowa Review, The New Republic, The New Yorker, The Paris Review, Poetry, The Yale Review,* and elsewhere. He has won various awards and prizes such as the Ohio State University Press / *The Journal* Award and the Lena-Miles Wever Todd Poetry Prize. He lives in Manhattan and Delaware County, New York, with his wife, the poet Roberta Swann.

Poetry Titles in the Series

John Hollander, *Blue Wine and Other Poems*
Robert Pack, *Waking to My Name: New and Selected Poems*
Philip Dacey, *The Boy under the Bed*
Wyatt Prunty, *The Times Between*
Barry Spacks, *Spacks Street, New and Selected Poems*
Gibbons Ruark, *Keeping Company*
David St. John, *Hush*
Wyatt Prunty, *What Women Know, What Men Believe*
Adrien Stoutenberg, *Land of Superior Mirages: New and Selected Poems*
John Hollander, *In Time and Place*
Charles Martin, *Steal the Bacon*
John Bricuth, *The Heisenberg Variations*
Tom Disch, *Yes, Let's: New and Selected Poems*
Wyatt Prunty, *Balance as Belief*
Tom Disch, *Dark Verses and Light*
Thomas Carper, *Fiddle Lane*
Emily Grosholz, *Eden*
X. J. Kennedy, *Dark Horses: New Poems*
Wyatt Prunty, *The Run of the House*
Robert Phillips, *Breakdown Lane*
Vicki Hearne, *The Parts of Light*
Timothy Steele, *The Color Wheel*
Josephine Jacobsen, *In the Crevice of Time: New and Collected Poems*
Thomas Carper, *From Nature*
John Burt, *Work without Hope: Poetry by John Burt*
Charles Martin, *What the Darkness Proposes: Poems*
Wyatt Prunty, *Since the Noon Mail Stopped*
William Jay Smith, *The World below the Window: Poems 1937–1997*
Wyatt Prunty, *Unarmed and Dangerous: New and Selected Poems*
Robert Phillips, *Spinach Days*
X. J. Kennedy, *The Lords of Misrule: Poems 1992–2001*
John T. Irwin, ed., *Words Brushed by Music: Twenty-Five Years of the Johns Hopkins Poetry Series*
John Bricuth, *As Long As It's Big: A Narrative Poem*
Robert Phillips, *Circumstances Beyond Our Control: Poems*
Daniel Anderson, *Drunk in Sunlight*
X. J. Kennedy, *In a Prominent Bar in Secaucus: New and Selected Poems, 1955–2007*
William Jay Smith, *Words by the Water*
Wyatt Prunty, *The Lover's Guide to Trapping*
Charles Martin, *Signs & Wonders*
Peter Filkins, *The View We're Granted*
Brian Swann, *In Late Light*